Edited by
BARBARA HOPKINSON

Norfolk in Colour

Photography and text by
Mark and Elizabeth Mitchels

Foreword by
Dick Joice

BARBARA HOPKINSON BOOKS

Acknowledgements

All the quotations in this book were written about Norfolk or by people who were either born here or spent a significant part of their lives in the county.

I am grateful to Mr J L Carr, novelist and publisher of poetry, unusual dictionaries and idiosyncratic maps, for allowing me to use some of the local sayings and pieces of poetry from his maps of Norfolk.

The photograph of Great Witchingham Hall is the copyright of Bernard Matthews PLC and is reproduced with their kind permission.

Barbara Hopkinson Books
Heron House
Low Road
Forncett St. Mary
Norwich NR16 1JJ
Tel: 050841 8367

ISBN 1 870632 00 1

Introduction

There is something peculiarly English about our attitude to Norfolk in that while both of us have enjoyed our explorations of the county, we have never quite lost that twinge of conscience which questions the wisdom of encouraging others to savour its pleasures. England is strewn with beauty spots which have become eyesores, and great buildings which have had to exchange their dignity for a very necessary income from visitors. Sadly, those of us who sing the praises of unknown East Anglia must bear some of the blame for the growing number of tourists who take us at our word, but let us hope that, as in history, the East Anglian will change and absorb all invaders, while retaining his own sturdy independence.

Norfolk is a wonderfully varied county. First there is the coastline, which takes in the tourist pleasures of resorts like Great Yarmouth, and also includes the tranquillity of a nature reserve at a place such as Cley. Then there are the Broads, at times a high road of river craft intent on fun, while the same waters can provide an artist with a lifetime of inspiration. Norfolk may be considered flat in comparison with some other counties – but there are rolling hills, wooded valleys and a gentle kind of beauty. The market towns are a world away from the frenzied and impersonal activity of the city. Here the visitor encounters the strange accents, sensible people and extraordinary kindness which characterise this region.

The place of Norfolk in the history of this country is assured. In prehistoric times there were the flint miners of Grime's Graves; later, Boudicca, Queen of the Iceni, defended her kingdom against Roman greed; from the medieval period we have the castles and abbeys of the Norman conquerors who captured lands of prime agricultural importance. Indeed, at the time of the Domesday Book, Norfolk, Suffolk and Essex were so prosperous that they merited a volume of the survey to themselves. Sheep, and the trades associated with them, provided Norfolk with riches down the centuries, especially after the arrival of Flemish weavers whose superior skills increased England's wealth. In the 18th century Norwich adjusted to the decline of the wool trade and became a handsome regional capital. But the countryside continued to flourish, because at this time Coke of Holkham introduced his far-reaching changes to the techniques of farming, now seen as an agricultural revolution.

Other individuals, too, have left their mark: Mother Julian, whose mystical vision of Divine Love has inspired Christians across the years; Cotman and the Norwich School of Artists who preserved for us their view of Norfolk in the last century; Elizabeth Fry, the pioneer of prison reform; and, of course, Nelson, the supreme English hero whose legacy was this country's domination of 19th century trade.

But ultimately the fascination of Norfolk has little to do with spectacular historical events; it is found in a sense of steady and unbroken achievement beneath the wide Norfolk sky.

Mark and Elizabeth Mitchels

FOR PHILIP AND JOHN

Foreword

When, in 1982, Barbara Hopkinson asked me to write the foreword to her, then soon to be published, *Suffolk in Colour* we talked about a sequel for Norfolk. If I am absolutely honest I didn't think it would come along quite so soon, although having heard of the tremendous success of *Suffolk in Colour* I am not now surprised, for it turned out to be an extremely popular book. In the original foreword I said that having been brought up in Norfolk and educated in Suffolk I had to admit that the two counties were not all that different, but on reflection, certainly in some very basic ways, they are. For instance it isn't often realized that Norfolk has a West coast, albeit a short one, or that when you go due North from Norfolk you are not going anywhere else in Great Britain and will finally finish up at the North Pole – if you go far enough! In fact that is the reason that the coast from Hunstanton to Cromer was considered by the Victorians and Edwardians to be an extremely healthy place to live and beneficial particularly to those suffering from TB or, as it was then known, Consumption.

What does this large egg-shaped piece of England have to offer? It must be admitted that there is one thing it doesn't – mountains – however on the Wash, where King John is supposed to have lost his treasure (although King's Lynn has a few pieces of it), and where they now fish for, amongst other things cockles, is the side which joins Lincolnshire and the eastern boundary of Cambridgeshire. This is where it gets its reputation for being flat, for the north eastern railway from London comes up via Cambridge and the view the traveller gets of the county is a vast area of black land growing magnificent crops and known as the Fens.

Moving West from here Breckland soon changes the traveller's view, for Breckland is almost unique with its pine forests and Grimes Graves where 4000 years ago neolithic man mined flints for his axes and spears. This area is one of the most beautiful in England.

The whole of the centre of the county of the north folk (as opposed to the south folk), is still truly rural and will grow almost any crop from cereals and sugar beet to grapes for wine as well as bulbs and fruit.

At its widest part the county is 67 miles across and 43 the other way. Within its compass there is everything (except those mountains), although it is by no means all flat but gently undulates with its many rivers and valleys.

As well as its magnificent beaches, Norfolk boasts the unique Broads, a little bit too popular nowadays in high Summer; the road left to us by the Romans which runs from Ixworth in Suffolk to the Wash, known as Peddars Way; the big international ports of Great Yarmouth and King's Lynn and the smaller picturesque sea ports and fishing villages like Wells, Cromer and Sheringham.

But perhaps Norfolk's greatest pride is its stately homes and vast agricultural estates, Sandringham, Holkham, Raynham, Houghton and Wolterton with hundreds of splendid manor houses to go with them. It abounds with churches, mostly built of flint, that range from one of England's greatest cathedrals at Norwich, to the tiny Saxon church at Newton by Castle Acre. There is also a magnificent castle at Norwich and the ruins of others at Castle Rising, Castle Acre and Baconsthorpe.

However it is the people of Norfolk who have since Boadicea jealously guarded their heritage and made the county such a splendid and pleasing place for the likes of Mark and Elizabeth Mitchels to photograph, and for Barbara Hopkinson to produce such a lovely book. It is a pleasure to give it the highest possible recommendation and wish her the very best of luck with it. I am sure you will be as enthusiastic about the book as I am.

Dick Joice

Ode to the Northeast Wind

WELCOME, wild North-easter!
Shame it is to see
Odes to every zephyr;
Ne'er verse to thee.
Welcome, black North-easter!
O'er the German foam;
O'er the Danish moorlands.
From thy frozen home.
Tired we are of summer,
Tired of gaudy glare,
Showers soft and steaming,
Hot and breathless air.
Tired of listless dreaming,
Through the lazy day;
Jovial wind of winter
Turns us out to play!
Sweep the golden reed-beds;
Crisp the lazy dyke;
Hunger into madness
Every plunging pike.
Fill the lake with wild fowl;
Fill the marsh with snipe;
While on dreary moorlands
Lonely curlew pipe.
Through the black fir-forest
Thunder harsh and dry,
Shattering down the snow-flakes
Off the curdled sky.
Hark! the brave North-easter!
Breast-high lies the scent,
On by holt and headland,
Over heath and bent.
Chime, ye dappled darlings,
Through the sleet and snow,
Who can over-ride you?
While our skates are ringing
O'er the frozen streams.
Let the luscious South-wind
Breathe in lovers' sighs,
While the lazy gallants
Bask in ladies' eyes.
What does he but soften
Heart alike and pen?
Tis the hard grey weather
Breeds hard English men.
What's the soft South-wester?
'Tis the ladies' breeze,
Bringing home their true-loves
Out of all the seas:
But the black North-easter,
Through the snowstorm hurled,
Drives our English hearts of oak
Seaward round the world.
Come, as came our fathers,
Heralded by thee,
Conquering from the eastward.
Lords by land and sea.
Come; and strong within us
Stir the Vikings' blood;
Bracing brain and sinew;
Blow, thou wind of God!

Charles Kingsley 1819—1875

'Was there ever,' cried he, 'such stuff as great part of Shakespeare? Only one must not say so! But what think you? – what? – Is there not sad stuff? what? – what?'

King George III to Fanny Burney (in her Diary, 19th Dec. 1785)

Sandringham House (front cover)

For the majority of the population, Sandringham House is the place where the Royal Family spends its Winter holiday and annually both media and public swarm to the church gates on Christmas morning to catch a glimpse of the Queen and her family. Sandringham House is not a palace but rather a truly private residence.

It was the future Edward VII who bought the 7,000 acre estate in 1862 for £22,000, and set about transforming the modest shooting lodge into a large country house in the Jacobean style. The magnificent wrought-iron gates which guard the drive entrance were a wedding present to the Prince and his bride from the local gentry. In church, the king limited the sermons to a maximum of ten minutes and rarely stayed for the whole service. He was fond of jokes and amusement. The story is told that at one house party before the First World War he came upon a whiskered retainer by the roadside, to whom he introduced himself and his distinguished guests: 'I am the King of England, this is the German Kaiser, and this gentleman is the Tsar of all the Russias.' Unimpressed, the rustic replied, 'And I'm the Archbishop of Canterbury,' continuing on his way – much to the King's delight.

For King George V this was a favourite retreat and he gave it the warmest tribute possible: 'The place I love better than anywhere else in the world.' He died at the house in 1936, as did his son George VI in 1952.

The House and extensive grounds are open to the public from Easter until late September, unless the Royal family is in residence.

One, Kemp, came dancing all the way from London to Norwich, which at that time may be considered as a wonder, as there were then no public roads, nor any surveyors appointed to keep the beaten tracks in repair.

Recorded in an old history of Norwich as having taken place in 1599.

William Kemp was an actor and a friend of Shakespeare.

Norwich Cathedral at dusk

There is something satisfying about a cathedral spire; perhaps that is why the great builders vied with each other to reach ever closer to heaven. Salisbury is the tallest, but Norwich is a very graceful second at 315 feet.

The first stones of this building were laid in 1094 and the cathedral was completed in 1145, but the great glories of the roof and the spire date from the 15th century. Outside is a Close of perfect proportion and like the monks of old who once paced its stones in quiet meditation, the visitor today can ignore the busy world beyond. The sheer skill of the medieval architects is always breath-taking but at Norwich it is particularly so, for the ground on which the cathedral is built was marshy and unstable. Outside, at the east end, is the grave of Nurse Edith Cavell who died before a firing squad in 1915.

Beyond the great Erpingham Gate the Georgian elegance of Tombland is revealed; further towards the shopping centre and over the River Wensum is Magdalen Street, the medieval hub of the wool trade upon which this lovely city's prosperity was founded.

God moves in a mysterious way
His wonders to perform;
He plants his footsteps in the sea,
And rides upon the storm.

William Cowper 1731–1800

Mundesley Beach

There is something wonderfully Edwardian about Mundesley; it retains the power to suggest a vanished elegance, donkey rides along a sandy beach, sand castles and sea-side rock and the gentle sounds of music from the bandstand. In summer vast blue skies proclaim that this is holiday time and Mundesley offers sand, sea and relaxation.

The noted East Anglian poet William Cowper stayed in the High Street when he visited the coast, which he often did throughout his life. The religious and emotional upheavals he endured may have been made bearable by this splendid prospect.

Sumer is icumen in,
Llude sing cuccu!
Groweth sed and bloweth med,
And springth the wude nu.

First recorded by John Fornset. c. 1250

Pulham Market

This is more correctly described as Pulham St Mary Magdalene, if only to distinguish it from the nearby Pulham St Mary the Virgin. In the old days it did indeed have a market and it remains a settlement surrounded by farming communities and their property. The village green in spring fulfils every wish of the townsman for the country: the Crown Inn and the church seem to exist contentedly side by side, gazing at a cluster of lovely cottages each more perfect than the last.

The Crown Inn
PULHAM
MARKET

For though my ryme be ragged,
Tattered and jagged,
Rudely rayne-beaten,
Rusty and mothe-eaten,
If ye take well therwith,
It hath in it some pyth.

John Skelton 1460?–1529

Attleborough

There is a strong sense of the past in Attleborough, a small market town celebrated over hundreds of years for its cider and turkeys.

The Norman Church of St Mary possesses the finest rood loft and screen in England. A rood screen is so called because it is surmounted by a great crucifix or rood, which directs the attention of the congregation to the simple statement of faith which it symbolizes. The loft runs the length of the screen and while today the space is often occupied by an organ, in the past it was the place for the village musicians who led the singing in church.

It is thought that the road between Attleborough and Wymondham was the first turnpike to be made in England. In 1707 the highway was extended to Norwich and 50 years later a coach service began making the journey from Norwich to London in a day.

ATTLEBOROUGH

There was an old person of Cromer
Who stood on one leg to read Homer;
When he found he grew stiff, he jumped over the cliff
Which concluded that Person of Cromer.

Edward Lear 1812–1888

Cromer

The tower of St Peter and St Paul's Church stands 160 feet tall and before a lighthouse was built on this stretch of the coast, the tower provided the beacon for those in peril on the sea. The Cromer lifeboat is justly proud of its lifesaving record; during the Second World War it saved 450 seafarers and its best known son, Cox'n Henry Bloggs, was the most decorated lifeboatman in the country, gaining three RNLI Gold Medals, the British Empire Medal and the George Cross. His bravery and resourcefulness were the stuff of legend: rescuing the crew of the barge *Sepoy* he drove his boat through a wave and on to the deck of the barge itself, grabbing the crew as he crashed down the other side. He died in 1954 and his place was taken by his nephews.

The holiday-maker is well catered for at Cromer with its long, inviting beach, delightful streets and pier complete with variety entertainment. Cromer crabs are reputed to be the best in England and, when not serving on the lifeboats, the seamen pursue the task of supplying the ready market.

Felbrigg Hall, two miles to the south west, is a stylish Jacobean house set amid beautiful parklands.

R.N.L.I.

Sin is behovely, but all shall be well and all shall be well and all manner of thing shall be well.

Dame Julian of Norwich 1343–1443

A winter scene near Ditchingham

Sheep have been described as 'East Anglia's Golden Fleece' and so indeed they were, for many of the finest churches can trace their origins to a wealthy wool merchant whose fears for his immortal soul turned his thoughts heavenwards.

Ditchingham House was once the residence of Rider Haggard, the successful Victorian novelist and author of 'King Solomon's Mines,' 'She' and 'Alan Quartermain'.

Norfolk has known some notable women writers and the turn of the 18th century produced a number of intellectuals and philanthropists including Amelia Opie, Elizabeth Fry, Harriet Martineau, Anna Sewell and Fanny Burney.

In 14th century Norwich a lady wrote a book which was to become internationally acknowledged as one of the great works of religious experience. She suffered a severe illness, during the course of which she had sixteen visions of Christ. On recovering her health and as a result of her experience, she felt called to become an anchoress, spending the rest of her life in her cell, meditating on her visions and helping those in need of spiritual guidance. Her retreat is in King Street, adjoining St Julian's Church from which she took her name. Towards the end of her life she wrote 'Revelations of Divine Love', the first recorded book to have been written by an Englishwoman.

The sisters of the Anglican Community of nuns at Ditchingham tend the shrine of Mother Julian of Norwich, a peaceful oasis visited by thousands of pilgrims from all over the world.

Regarding Sir Edward Coke, Norfolk Solicitor. 1552–1634.
He left an estate of £11,000 pa. Sir Edward Danvers, who knew him, told me he had heard one say to him, reflecting on his great scraping of wealth, that his sonnes would spend his estate faster than he gotte it; he replyed, 'They cannot take more delight in the spending of it than I did in the getting of it.'

John Aubrey in Brief Lives

Pull's Ferry, Norwich

Building Norwich cathedral was a formidable enough task without the additional problem of carrying the stone from the river's edge. The monks themselves are reputed to have built this canal to bring Caen stone right up to the site. There were three gateways to the cathedral close, but this watergate of flint and stone was probably the most widely used. A ferry house was built beside it.

Towards the end of the 12th century there were three stone buildings in the City of Norwich, the Cathedral, the Castle and the Music House, then known as the house of Jurnet the Jew, one of the wealthiest men in the city. He and his fellow money-lenders provided capital for the King and overlords to carry out their ambitious plans. The Jews were dispossessed by King John and the house eventually passed into the hands of the Paston family. Now known as Wensum Lodge, it is a centre for continuing education.

The name of the ferry is taken from that of an 18th century ferryman who worked this part of the river.

'Caister men never turn back'.

The reply made by a member of the lifeboat crew during the Inquiry held in 1901 into an obviously hopeless rescue attempt.

Caister Castle

Sir John Fastolfe (1378–1459) was one of the 'happy few' who in 1415 stood beside King Henry V at Agincourt and won a famous victory. When he returned to his estates in Norfolk, he used his military experience to design a castle able to withstand the assaults of his many enemies. His work remains today, at least in part, especially the round tower 98 feet high with a stair turret at the side. But what makes his memory the fonder with historians is that he kept every document to do with the castle's construction and use. Such a collection is unusual but Caister Castle was next occupied by an even more famous family of letter writers – the Pastons, who lived (and withstood sieges) here in the 15th and 16th centuries. The letters between Margaret and her husband John Paston remain an invaluable record of life for a family in the troubled times of the Wars of the Roses.

The castle is open to the public and provides history in two very different forms, as in addition to the medieval castle there is a motor museum of vintage cars and motor cycles which should evoke memories for many visitors, although few could have seen the 1904 steam powered car in action.

There is a spectacular view of the coastline from the top of the brick tower.

Farewell rewards and fairies,
Good housewives now may say,
For now, foul sluts in dairies,
So fare as well as they,
And though they sweep their hearths no less
Than maids were wont to do,
Yet who, of late, for cleanliness
Finds sixpence in her shoe?

Richard Corbet, Bishop of Norwich 1582–1635
lamenting Puritanical influence

The Church at Walpole St Peter

East Anglia is full of villages where one looks at the church and wonders why it is so enormous. Can there ever have been a time when so many people lived and worked there? The church at Walpole St Peter evokes such questions, for it is quite simply the most wonderful, huge and awe-inspiring edifice any city could wish to possess – and it stands in a small, attractive village about four miles from the Wash. This church, which vies with that of Terrington St Clement for the title of 'the Cathedral of the Fens', was probably the victim of history. Many churches like this stand witness to the terrible effect of the Black Death upon its citizens and its prosperity.

The interior is beautifully proportioned and bathed in clear light from the graceful Perpendicular windows. The altar has the unusual feature of being raised and approached by nine steps. It is thought that this was to allow continued access to the 'Bolt Hole', a passage below the East end of the church and a medieval right of way. A guide to English churches selects Walpole St Peter as 'surely the most beautiful parish church interior' and it is difficult to disagree.

Here Ouse, slow winding through a level plain
Of spacious meads with cattle sprinkled o'er,
Conducts the eye along its sinuous course
Delighted . . .

William Cowper 1731–1800 From *The Task*

Denver Sluice

It is no exaggeration to say that these sluice gates protect the lives of thousands of people; without them, an enormous inland area would regularly be flooded by the sea tides racing up the Great Ouse river. The tidal range in the Wash can be as much as 18 feet at certain times of the year; only these gates and the high banks of the rivers safeguard the inhabitants of this stark landscape.

The Dutch engineer Vermuyden was the first to construct a system of dams to hold back the tides but much of his work was destroyed by the 'Sea Tigers' – fenmen whose living depended on the eeling and wildfowling he threatened. Eventually the work was completed and among the beneficiaries was the modern port of King's Lynn, which owes its importance to its location at the head of so many controlled waterways. The Great Ouse river is navigable inland as far as Bedford.

The Denver Sluice project was finished in 1959 and marks the point at which the Ouse is joined by the New Bedford River.

St. Denis for France, St. James for Spaine,
St. Patrike for Ireland, St. George for England
and the red herring for Yarmouth.

Thomas Nashe 1567–1601

Great Yarmouth

Herring were the life blood of this great fishing port and even into the 20th century the Scottish girls' arrival would herald another crop from the sea, to be gutted and prepared for the tables of the land. The golden days of the Herring Fair were just before the First World War but they stretched back to the Middle Ages, when the Free Herring Fair was renowned as one of England's greatest trade fairs. The last drifter was sold in 1963 and while there is still a fishing fleet based here, it now seeks for fish hundreds of miles over the horizon and often far to the north. Today Great Yarmouth is bustling with the latest technology, for it was the first base for the discovery of North Sea Gas and oil and many erstwhile fishermen are now to be found on tugs, supply boats and drilling platforms.

The holiday centre of Great Yarmouth is ideally suited to the visitors, for in addition to a seafront of four miles – much of it sandy beach – there is a first class pier theatre attracting many popular entertainers and the nightlife is geared to ensure that no one leaves without happy memories.

The town derives its name from the River Yare which joins the sea at this place. It occupies a narrow peninsula which accounts for the mass of little lanes, the Rows, which form a grid throughout the town. There were once supposed to be 145 of them, and the width of the smallest is said to be only 30 inches. Many were destroyed by bombs in the last war. Nelson's battle fleets anchored here during the Napoleonic wars and there is a very interesting Maritime Museum on the sea front which documents the naval history of the area. The town also possesses many ancient and fascinating buildings.

BRITANNIA THEATRE
PROFESSOR RICHARDSON'S POPULAR
PUNCH & JUDY
NEXT SHOW.
11 30
TRADITIONAL
SHOW
25 P.

To a New York trader I did belong
She was built for sea, both stout and strong,
Well rigged, well manned, well fit for sea;
She was bound for New York in Ameriky.

Norfolk Song *The Norfolk Trader*

King's Lynn

King's Lynn is exactly what it appears to be: an ancient port serving the many towns which lie far inland and depending upon it for access to the markets of Britain and Europe. It was once called Bishop's Lynn but royal patronage from Henry VIII resulted in the change of name and heightened status.

The king most associated with this town is King John, who presented the Corporation with an embossed and enamelled cup and cover of silver. It is the earliest piece of English medieval secular plate and very beautiful. In October 1215, still smarting from his enforced signing of the Magna Carta, King John left Lynn for Newark rashly opting to take the short cut across the Fens. The locals warned him but, unheeding, he continued and too late saw his crown jewels and treasury sink beneath the incoming tide. Some sceptics have suspected John of creating this legend to justify increased taxation. Nevertheless, even today there are figures with metal-detectors to be seen sweeping the mud-flats at low water.

King's Lynn is one of those places which must be explored on foot. Once you discover the streets of this port you wonder how so much of it has survived. The answer is often that one of the thriving local heritage groups has done a wonderful job of preserving the best. The Greenland Fishery House of 1605 is but one of a clutch of perfectly-restored merchants' residences, giving an insight into the wealth of the town.

The Custom House is the most photogenic building in the port; it occupies the east bank of the Ouse and still stands only yards away from the maritime trade it served. The House was designed by Henry Bell in 1683, influenced by the Dutch style popular at that time throughout East Anglia; originally the ground floor was open and used for trading by the merchants.

The two Guild Halls are rivals with the Custom House for the title of Lynn's most distinguished building, and it would be a brave soul who offered a view. Suffice to say that King's Lynn is extraordinarily fortunate to possess such a trio. The Guildhall of the Holy Trinity dates from 1421 and with its chequered flint and stone flushwork proclaims the civic pride which inspired it – and the wealth which could afford it.

Sow beans and peas on David and Chad
Be the weather good or bad.

Trad.

After the Harvest

Norfolk is a county for those who like their skies to be large and open; the brilliance of light is often breath-taking. To cross the land at dusk is to behold richer colours than exist on any artist's palette, and the sunsets are spectacular.

While the Suffolk Punch is naturally associated with the southern neighbour, Norfolk too has a history of dependence on sturdy horses and a few remain of the thousands who toiled in field and lane.

Return, sweet Evening and continue long!
Methinks I see thee in the streaky West,
With matron-step slow moving, while the night
Treads on thy sweeping train . . .

William Cowper 1731–1800

Blakeney at Sunset

There is something entirely welcoming about any place which is the haunt of yachtsmen, wildfowlers and naturalists; Blakeney can claim to be all three. This picturesque one-time port possessed a superb natural harbour of the sort much in demand centuries ago when ships needed only shallow draught and road transport was slow, expensive and risky. A deep water anchorage exists close by, a mere three miles downstream. It is called the Pit, giving a clue to the sudden increased depth of water experienced at this point.

Many of the port buildings are of flint, a widely used local material and one which has taxed the ingenuity of builders for hundreds of years, with pleasing results.

For the nature lover this region abounds in interest. The National Trust Reserve is perfectly sited for botanists and birdwatchers, being surrounded by sand dunes, salt marshes and mud flats. The more fortunate – or observant – can even spot seals at the right time of the year.

'Very flat, Norfolk'

Noel Coward *Private Lives*

Burgh Castle

During the third century AD the Romans found this island under attack from invaders – Anglo Saxons from northern Germany. As the raiders grew bolder with each success, serious attention was given to the task of holding the eastern shores. A line of forts was constructed from Portchester on the south coast to Branchester near the Wash. Burgh Castle was sited to protect the Roman town of Caistor, which is thought to have been Gariannonum. Here would have been anchored a Roman fleet of fast galleys available to intercept raids along this part of the coast. Giant catapults would have been mounted on the bastions, or towers, which line the massive walls of flint and which are strengthened by seams of brick.

More peaceful use was made of the site soon after, for it became an Anglo Saxon monastery. Later a Norman motte and bailey castle was built in the southern corner of the inner wall area; nothing of these now remains. Only in 1846 was the fort saved from constant quarrying when it was purchased and preserved, being given to the State in 1929.

Across the water where once a fleet of war galleys rocked at anchor, can be seen the Berney Arms Windpump, which once helped to drain the land; it is still in working order and open to visitors.

Rising was a seaport when Lynn was but a marsh,
Now Lynn it is a seaport and Rising fares the worse.

Anon.

Castle Rising

As is so often the case doggerel verse encapsulates the truth, for it was the silting up of the River Babington which curtailed the prosperity of Castle Rising at a time when King's Lynn was becoming the major trading centre of the region.

The spectacular castle stands within a massive earthwork which may date from Roman times. Built in 1150 by William de Albini, it consists of a squat Hall-Keep of two storeys surrounded by a rampart 1000 yards in circumference and as much as 64 feet high. All these fortifications were largely wasted, however, as there is no evidence that the castle was ever called upon to withstand a siege.

The castle's most famous resident was more a prisoner than a guest. Isabella of France was the wife of Edward II, whom she despised; she had a very public affair with Roger Mortimer, which culminated in the imprisonment and murder of her royal husband and the proclamation of her thirteen year old son as Edward III. Two years later, the boy struck back; in 1330 Mortimer was seized and executed and Isabella was sent to Castle Rising, there to end her days , occasionally enlivened by news of the exploits of her son and his even more renowned offspring, the Black Prince. They visited her at the castle. Long after her death 'the she-wolf of France' was supposed to haunt the castle, but now it has a decidedly unthreatening atmosphere.

Nearby is the Trinity Hospital, or Bede House, a group of 17th century almshouses set around a courtyard. On Sundays the elderly ladies wear their scarlet cloaks embroidered with the Howard badge in memory of their benefactor, the Duke of Norfolk; on the Founder's birthday they wear black conical hats. The rules set down for the eleven residents are clear about the qualifications for entry, requiring them to be 'of honest life and conversation, religious, grave and discreet, able to read if such a one may be had, single, 56 at least, no common beggar, harlot, scold, drunkard, haunter of taverns, inns or alehouses'.

The past is another country; they do things differently there.

L P Hartley *The Go-Between*

Hunstanton

This town was created in the Edwardian era as a seaside resort, and has the interesting distinction of being the only one in East Anglia to face westward.

Some of the first people to reach this part of the coast would have travelled along the Peddar's Way – an ancient track dating from unwritten history – which ends here. The Le Strange family were the local landowners in the 19th century, and the arrival of the railway spurred them to create a holiday retreat in the shadow of these most unusual cliffs, striped with chalk, clay, stone and sand. The Le Stranges kept a firm grasp on the property, however, and to this day claim the right to any oysters and mussels taken from the foreshore.

The town is delightful, possessing all the traditional qualities of a family resort. The elegant chateau-style houses proclaim a confidence and a gentility entirely becoming to this special part of Norfolk.

Bitter, bitter, oh to behould the grasse to growe
Where the walls of Walsingham so stately did show,
Levell, levell with the ground the towres do lye
Which with their golden glittering tops pearsed once to the skye.
Where were gates, no gates are nowe; the waies are unknown . . .

Anon.

Walsingham

In 1061 Lady Richeldis de Faverches saw in a dream the Virgin Mary, who told her to construct a replica of the holy house at Nazareth on her estate at Walsingham. Springs of water appeared to indicate the site, and the first of many chapels was built. Throughout the Middle Ages Walsingham was the greatest sacred place for pilgrims and became known as England's Nazareth. From the time of Richard the Lionheart onwards, few sovereigns neglected to pay their respects at the shrine; Henry VIII visited it before his greed led him to repudiate such beliefs, whereupon the statue of the Virgin Mary was taken to London and burned.

The Augustines founded a Priory here in 1149, but only the east window of the church survives. The grounds are themselves a vast gathering place for the twentieth century pilgrims who continue to pour into the town for religious festivals.

Walsingham itself is prettily situated in a valley. The village has a quaint central square surrounded by half-timbered buildings. It is at its most attractive when seen swarming with pilgrims, banners waving and bands playing, proclaiming their faith.

Malicious tunges, though they have no bones,
Are sharper than swordes, sturdier than stones.

John Skelton 1460–1529

Barton Broad

In their modest way the Norfolk Broads are worthy to be compared with the Pyramids of Egypt and the Great Wall of China, for like these more famous achievements of Man the Broads, too, were the work of men over hundreds of years. In medieval times this part of East Anglia was a source of peat, there being no coal nearby, and for centuries it was dug for fuel. Gradually the waters flowed in and thus were created the Broads, miles and miles of them, linked by cuts and channels. Now they are used by holiday makers and a thriving reed and cane industry but peat continues to be dug. Barton Broad is almost unapproachable by road, which makes it even more delightful for the few travellers who push boldly through the reeds to discover the beauty that awaits the last few footsteps to the water's edge. West of this point is the tiny village of Barton Turf, whose church has an impressive rood screen showing paintings of the Nine Orders of Angels, together with assorted saints and interesting pictures of four kings: Henry VI, Edmund the Martyr, Edward the Confessor and the delightfully named King Holofius, who does indeed hold a whole loaf.

TOBER

If Old England you would win
Then at Weybourne Hoop begin.

Anon. Said to have arisen at the time of the Spanish Armada in expectation of a landing there.

The Mill at Cley

In the medieval period Cley was a busy port with boats tied up alongside harbour walls; now it is some distance from the sea, and has a sad, nostalgic appearance which is perhaps understandable. The real blow to the port's prosperity came in the 17th century, when efforts to reclaim marshland conflicted with the need to keep the waterways open, and the seamen lost.

It is a village of sturdy flint houses, some of them quite old, but the central attraction is the 18th century windmill, which stands beside what was once the quayside. It is now open to the public.

St Margaret's church, which dates from the 14th century, affords another insight into the unpredictability of fortune: in expectation of continuing prosperity, the town began a great church which it found impossible to complete following the ravages of the Black Death in the mid-century.

Cley Marshes, purchased in 1926, were the very first property of the National Trust, and to this day their 650 acres of nature reserve are the goal of legions of dedicated bird watchers.

The Rose both White and Red
In one Rose now doth grow;
Thus thorough every sted
Thereof the fame doth blow.
Grace the seed did sow:
England, now gather floures,
Exclude now all doloures.

John Skelton 1460?–1529

Castle Acre Priory

In the years following the Norman conquest, William de Warenne built a castle on this site, the ruins of which remain, grandly topping the motte constructed to receive it. His son established a Cluniac priory close by, which had about thirty monks in it for most of its life, although at the time of the 16th century Dissolution this number had fallen to eleven. What survives now is a pleasant mixture of styles and buildings, including a gatehouse which became a farmer's family home. It is probably too fanciful to suggest that a life of contemplation appears to have left a permanent mark on the ruins, but they are beautiful and exude a peaceful contentment.

The village of Castle Acre lies on the ancient Peddar's Way, and is heralded by a quite remarkable village sign of a quality which only Norfolk seems to inspire. The great Bailey Gate dates from the early 13th century and still spans the village street.

Cromer crabs, Runton dabs,
Beeston babies, Sherringham ladies,
Weybourne witches, Salthouse ditches,
Blakeney bulldogs, Binham bulls,
Morston dodmen, Stiffkey trolls.

Trad.

Sheringham

This is offshore fishing country and the lobster and crab caught in these seas are destined for some very grand tables, as well as more humble boards in the caravans which dispense their treasures from Norfolk lay-bys. The Sheringham crab boat is small, double-ended and clinker built, an ageless triumph of experience and the builder's craft. Baited pots are strung out in a line on the fishing grounds off shore and hauled back up the next day, in a manoeuvre calling for skill and perfect timing of the tide.

The town is also a holiday resort and its narrow streets welcome the hordes of visitors with friendly pleasure. Chief among the attraction is the North Norfolk Railway, three miles of the former Midland and Great Northern circuit, now enthusiastically managed by volunteers. Running from the unspoilt 19th century station in the centre of Sheringham, the track follows the coastline to Weybourne. Even if you have never been here you may well have seen the line and stations as they often appear in films.

Thank God, I have done my duty.

Horatio, Lord Nelson 1758–1805

Burnham Thorpe

Occasionally someone who achieves world-wide fame is born in a village which would otherwise remain unknown. This is Nelson's birthplace and proud to be so. For miles around the pubs echo his story with such stirring names at *Victory*, *Trafalgar* and *Hero* but Burnham Thorpe is where he belongs. The rectory where he was born has now gone; however the Church of All Saints can claim to have seen his baptism and to have watched him grow from boy to man to legend. Nelson left this place in 1770 at the age of twelve to begin his career on the ship of his uncle, Captain Suckling. The rest is history.

Burnham Thorpe has not made an industry out of its hero, although it can show the lecturn in the church made from *Victory's* oak and Nelson Hall near by has a display of small relics. But the victories are not of this place and must be sought elsewhere; the local people are satisfied to think that the village shaped his beginnings.

The flag always flies from the church tower on October 21st, the anniversary of the Battle of Trafalgar, Nelson's greatest and final victory.

LORD NELSON
GREENE KING

My country is the world and my religion to do good.

Tom Paine 1737–1809

Thetford – Tom Paine's Statue

Thetford is a very ancient town. The Icknield Way, one of the prehistoric trackways, passes through it and it is spoken of as the capital of the Iceni tribe at the time of their revolt, led by Queen Boudicca, against the Romans. At one point it was the seat of the bishopric and the town's eminence is illustrated by the presence here of a nunnery, a priory and a monastery, now impressive ruins. Throughout the medieval period Thetford was a thriving centre for religious and commercial activity. When the religious establishments were closed in the 16th century, the town received a blow from which it never really recovered. Nevertheless, there are some fine old buildings to be seen, notably the Bell Hotel and the former gaol and Thetford is still an important shopping centre, straddling the rivers Thet and Little Ouse.

Tom Paine was born in 1737 at Grey Gables, then a small cottage. After a time as a minor official, he went to America, where his writings played no small part in encouraging the colonists to take the road to revolution. Returning to England he published 'The Rights of Man' (1791), but his views were regarded as treasonable and he was forced to flee to Revolutionary France. Even there his ideas on liberty and democracy were too strong and he went back to America, where he died in 1809. His most memorable phrase is not entirely divorced from his own experience: 'The sublime and the ridiculous are often so nearly related that it is difficult to class them separately'. The statue of Paine is by Charles Wheeler, and was presented to the town by the Tom Paine Society of the United States.

Thetford is surrounded by heath and woodland; Thetford Forest covers 83 square miles, making it the second largest forest in England. West of the town are the prehistoric flint mines known as Grimes' Graves.

1737 THOMAS PAINE 1809

This world is a comedy to those that think,
a tragedy to those that feel.

Horace Walpole, 4th Earl of Orford. 1717–1797

Blickling Hall

There are some views which really do take the breath away and Blickling is assuredly one. It has a perfection which is immediately impressive; what is more the spectacular view across the lawns towards the rich warm brick house is only a side view.

The house was built for Sir Henry Hobart by Robert Lyminge between 1616 and 1624, on the estate once owned by Sir John Fastolfe. The house as seen now is the result of substantial alterations in the late 18th century. Within there are ornate chimney pieces, plaster ceilings of infinite craftsmanship and a long gallery that is worth a visit for itself alone. This great room is almost 130 feet long, with windows on one side only, casting a light on a summer's day which kindles envy of those who once lived within.

The house is not only possessed of a superb collection of furniture, pictures and tapestries, but also comprises a workshop where works of art from all over East Anglia are brought for repair.

The gardens of Blickling on a summer's day are worthy of the house, being formal but intimate. Around a crescent-shaped lake are to be found neatly clipped hedges, an orangery and a temple. In all there is an air of timeless grace which would permit the visitor to come upon an 18th century scene with no more surprise or unease that that occasioned by the unexpected arrival of old and familiar friends.

Aylesham, near by, was once the centre of the weaving industry, and in the 18th century became a spa town. It is now a market town and has an attractive street plan of interesting buildings.

Here lies John Rackett,
In his wooden jacket;
He kept neither horses nor mules.
He lived like a hog,
And died like a dog,
And left all his money to fools.

From a nearby Burial Ground

January sun at Hempnall Ford

Hempnall is a small village, widely scattered and almost totally devoted to agriculture. It appears to be quite deserted and forgotten but only 100 years ago it was a thriving community of over 1,000 people served by many tradesmen including a clock-maker, a basket weaver, a barrel maker and no less than three tailors and five boot makers.

This treatise devysed it is
Of two knaves somtyme of Dis.

Though this knaves be deade,
Full of myschiefe and queed, (queed = evil)
Yet, where so ever they ly
Theyr names shall never dye.

Compendium de duobus versipellibus, John Jayberd et Adam all a knave, deque illorum notissima vilitate.

John Skelton 1460?–1529

The Mere at Diss

This six acre expanse of water predates the town, because the latter takes its name from the Anglo-Saxon word 'dice', meaning standing water.

The town retains its Tudor charm, being set around a market square half way up a hill and contains a delightful warren of small streets, many of which lead to a large green. John Skelton, poet and tutor to King Henry VIII, was Rector of St Mary's Church. A later poet, Sir John Betjeman, regarded this as his favourite Norfolk town.

The church was founded by Sir Robert Fitzwalter, a knight of high reputation in the reign of King John. The story goes that the monarch took a fancy to Matilda, the knight's fair daughter, and when his lust was frustrated by the protective father he became vengeful, banishing the poor man and poisoning the lady.

Shakespeare

January 28th 1780 . . . *The Company present were Sir Edmund Bacon and Lady, Mr. and Mrs. Custance and Mr. Press Custance . . . We had for diner a Calf's Head, boiled Fowl and Tongue, a Saddle of Mutton rosted on the Side Table, and a fine Swan rosted with Currant Jelly for the First Course. The Second Course a couple of Wild Fowl called Dun Fowls, Larks, Blamange, Tarts etc etc and a good Dessert of Fruit after, amongst which was a Damson Cheese. I never eat a bit of Swan before, and I think it good eating with sweet sauce. . .*

The Reverend James Woodforde 1740–1803
Rector of Weston Longville

Bishop Bonner's Cottages, East Dereham

These cottages beside St Withburga's Church have all the air of idyllic isolation from the world's turbulent affairs; the impression can be misleading for here lived Bonner, Rector of this parish from 1534 until 1540, who enjoyed advancement under the Catholic Queen Mary. He became Bishop of London and in that capacity was in the forefront of the attempt to crush the Protestant faith and return the country to its old allegiance to the Pope. He condemned many to the horrors of burning in the fires of Smithfield. The houses are now a Museum. The delicate and colourful plaster ornamentation called pargetry, is uncommon in Norfolk.

St Withburga was a daughter of the Anglo Saxon king, Anna, and set up a nunnery here in 650. Legend records that the nuns were so poor they were only fed by two does who came regularly to be milked. Unfortunately the town bailiff: 'envying them this supply, most maliciously hunted them away with his hounds; and as a just punishment upon him, he soon after broke his neck, as he was pursuing his favourite diversion of hunting'. So pious was St Withburga that when she died her body was stolen by the monks at Ely to encourage pilgrims to visit their cathedral.

East Dereham is a quiet, dignified town, and behind many of the more modern shop fronts there remain elegant 18th century residences.

Just outside the town is Quebec Hall, built in 1759 by Samuel Rash to celebrate one great victory in that year of victories (and Nelson's flagship was named to commemorate the fact). The woods around the Hall are laid out to recreate the dispositions adopted by the British and French armies on that far-off Canadian battlefield.

Streams never flow in vain; where streams abound,
How laughs the land with various plenty crown'd!
But time that should enrich the nobler mind,
Neglected, leaves a dreary waste behind.

William Cowper 1731–1800

Rollesby Broad

This is a rather unusual Broad because it is isolated from the main system and along with Ormesby Broad, exists on its own. The delightfully named Muck Fleet having silted up, the waterway which linked Rollesby and Ormesby to the whole Broadland network was thus obstructed. This means fewer cruising boats and more sailing craft. Roads cross the Broads here and allow easy access to picnic places with unrivalled views of the lovely expanse of water.

There is a gray old Castle upon the top of that mighty mound; and yonder, rising 300 feet above the soil, from among those noble forest trees, behold that old Norman master-work, that cloud encircled cathedral spire, around which a garrulous army of rooks and choughs continually wheel their flight.

George Borrow 1803–1881

Norwich Castle by Night

Norwich is justly proud of its appearance, and to see it at night is to experience a wealth of majestic buildings illuminated skilfully to great effect. The Castle Keep dominates every view of the city – more so than the Cathedral. That is as the builders of the fortress intended it should be.

Since the first days of Anglo-Saxon settlement Norwich has been a centre for trade and government. By the time of the Norman conquest it is said to have been one of the four great cities of England. It was an obvious choice for a regional centre and when the first Normans rode through the city gateway, the site for the castle was selected. 100 houses had the misfortune to be on the high ground already, but they soon were no more. The stone keep was probably constructed soon after 1100 and rose to a height of 70 feet from a 100 feet base. The outer stone facing seen today is, sadly, the result of Victorian restoration. In 1220 the soldiers marched out and the castle became the city's gaol and so it remained until 1887. It is now a well-presented Museum and Art Gallery, including among its treasures many examples of the Norwich School of painting.

From the summit a truly impressive view of this beautiful city is revealed. 'A church for every week; a pub for every day' goes the jingle, and it could well be true. Many of the churches have been taken over by more modern concerns, as the cost of keeping them in repair has proved too much for their falling congregations. Two have provided homes for the Norwich Art Centre and the Norwich Puppet Theatre while the city's three other theatres, the Maddermarket, the Sewell Barn and the Theatre Royal, whose origins date back to 1757, play to audiences in more worldly surroundings.

Turkey, heresy, hops and beer came to England all in one year.

Anon.

Great Witchingham Hall

Great Witchingham Hall is set in the heart of beautiful North Norfolk countryside. The foundations of the hall were laid in the 16th century with the building of the original moated Tudor manor house. Considerable additions were made to the residence in the 18th century. The majestic red brick mansion has embattled towers and octagonal turrets with shaped finials at every angle of the building.

Bernard Matthews bought the property in 1955 for what today seems the very modest sum of £3,000 and gradually began extensive renovation to restore it to its former beauty. Now the transformation is complete, with gardens and parkland coaxed back to their earlier glory.

For centuries Norfolk has been celebrated for its magnificent turkeys and the largest most advanced turkey farm in Europe is centred at this great hall, now the headquarters of the Bernard Matthews organisation. In the early days of the business, most of the vast mansion was occupied by turkeys, the owners themselves using only four rooms; the last of the turkeys departed from the hall many years ago and the majority of the rooms have been converted into offices.

Introduced to England in the 1530s from America, the turkey rapidly became traditional Christmas fare. In those days the flocks would set off in August to walk to London, often having their feet covered with tar to prevent them becoming sore on the journey; they ate and rested en route at time honoured places. Since we now eat turkey all the year round, it is as well that more efficient modes of transport have evolved.

Today it is well, tomorowe it is all amysse;
Today in delyte, tomorowe bare of blysse;
Today a lorde, tomorowe ly in the duste:
Thus in this worlde there is no erthly truste

Today fayre wether, tomorowe a stormy rage;
Today hote, tomorowe outragyous colde;
Today a yoman, tomorowe made of page;
Today in surety, tomorowe bought and solde;
Today maysterfest, tomorowe he hath no holde; *(maysterfest = bound to a master)*
Today a man, tomorowe he lyeth in the duste:
Thus in this worlde there is no erthly truste.

John Skelton 1460?–1529

East Barsham Hall

This is a place to discover on a late summer's evening, for at that time the declining sun picks out the rich colours of the brickwork and highlights the sheer exuberance of the chimneys and statuary. The house was built by Sir Henry Fermor in about 1525 but there must have been an estate here before then, as Henry VIII is reputed to have stayed at East Barsham and walked barefoot to the shrine of Our Lady at Walsingham in 1511.

What is seen today has been heavily restored and the high walls around the house lure the visitor with a skyline of intriguing complexity and grandeur.

Thus we are men and we know not how;
there is something in us that can be without us.

Sir Thomas Browne 1605–1682

Wymondham Abbey Church

The Abbey was founded in 1107 by William, Earl of Arundel and among its first endowments received this curious one from King Henry I: 'all wrecks on that part of the coast lying between Eccles, Happisburgh and Tunstead, and a rent in kind of 2000 eels annually from the village of Hilgay'. Church and town were soon at loggerheads and so they remained for the life of the Abbey. The dispute produced an expensive farce in the 15th century for, when the Abbey was divided between the monks and the townspeople, the former built a grand octagonal tower at the present East end and a wall across the nave, thereby destroying the townspeople's view of the High altar. Indignantly, the parish retaliated by building an even grander tower at the West end. The interior of the church possesses a beautiful hammerbeam roof but most of the rest of the Abbey was destroyed by the town after the Dissolution.

The town of Wymondham suffered badly from a fire in the early 17th century, and so most of the buildings around the square reflect the taste and styles of the 18th century. The octagonal market cross has an open ground floor, and an outside staircase leading to a timbered upper room; the effect is most pleasing.

The Kett brothers who raised an unsuccessful rebellion against land enclosures and other encroachments of the rights of the poor, were tanners of Wymondham. A contemporary report of their defeat in 1549 runs 'Robert Ket of Mousehold Heath strung up at Norwich Castle and his brother William dangling from Wymondham steeple'.

My favourite, I might say, my only study, is man.

George Borrow 1803–1881

The River Ant near Ludham Bridge

Ludham occupies a commanding view over three Norfolk rivers, the Thurne, Bure and Ant. The old trades and crafts have almost gone, as now the river welcomes thousands of pleasure craft and holiday-makers intent on forgetting the pressure of the world beyond these beautiful stretches of reed-lined water. A similar desire for tranquility and contemplation must have led the monks of St Benet's Abbey to establish their retreat beside the Bure, in an almost inaccessible position a few miles away. The Bishop of Norwich still visits the ruined site once a year, in August, and conducts a service. As the sound of voices floats across the water on a late summer evening, there must be a stir of memory among the long departed souls of all who have found this place a sanctuary.

From Ludham Bridge the spectator can indulge in a popular riverside activity: laughing at the errors of the inexperienced helmsman who but a week ago was happily distant from all things maritime.

Good ale, the true and proper drink of Englishmen. He is not deserving of the name of Englishman who speaketh against ale, that is good ale.

George Borrow 1803–1881

Swaffham

There are worse fates for towns than being the subjects of folk tales, so Swaffham wears its fame with pride. The legend concerns John Chapman, a pedlar, who dreamt that if he went to London and stood on London Bridge he would discover a fortune. Off he went, and for days paced the length of the bridge without success. Eventually a man who had observed his curious behaviour spoke to him and, hearing about the dream, told the story of a dream he himself had experienced but intended to ignore. The pedlar was amazed, for the man's dream was meant to be heard by him. 'I dreamt that at a place called Swaffham, in Norfolk, dwells John Chapman, a pedlar, who hath a tree at the back of his house under which is buried a pot of gold.' And so it proved to be. The Church of St Peter and St Paul in Swaffham does indeed have gifts from John Chapman dating from the mid 15th century, and the same man donated £120 towards the building of the spire, but some people continue to doubt the whole story.

At the opposite end of the wide market place stands the domed rotunda, built in 1783 from a donation by the Earl of Orford. It serves as a market cross, and is surmounted by a fine statue of Ceres, holding a sheaf of corn. Around the market place are many outstanding buildings, some of them dating from the prosperous 18th century. The town continues to be a busy market centre for the region; five roads converge at the elegant rotunda, and the consequent bustle and activity delight the visitor with their cheerful industry.

SWAFFHAM
Ye pedlar of Swaffham
who did by a dream
find a great treasure
KINGS ARMS
MITCHELL

Youth will be served, every dog has his day, and mine has been a fine one.

George Borrow 1803–1881

Coltishall

This place marks the navigable limit of the River Bure and it serves as a shooting and angling centre for the waters around. Boating has easily joined these time-honoured pursuits, and for many holiday-makers Coltishall is their entry point to the Broads. A wide grassy area between river and road tempts the visitor to stop and survey the pleasure boats moored alongside.

The village has a number of fine 18th century buildings, and the church of St John the Baptist has a thatched roof.

Hemp seed I set. Hemp seed I sow.
He that will my true love be,
Come after me – and mow.

Trad.

Fakenham

Seen from the south, Fakenham is dominated by the tower of the Church of St Peter and St Paul.

The town is of Anglo-Saxon foundation but the predominant architectural impression is of an 18th century market town, revolving around the market place and based on the tap rooms of the two coaching inns which front the central square. This is a charming English provincial town in the best sense.

Times go by turns, and chances change by course,
From foul to fair, from better hap to worse.

Robert Southwell 1561?–1595

Downham Market

Situated on the very edge of fen country, Downham Market was an obvious market place for the region's produce. It had the extra advantage of direct river access to the sea and so flourished. The trade boom and the sense of comfort it fostered are well attested to by the lines of mellow carrstone buildings which characterise its quiet streets. The arrival of the railway was a cruel blow because it cut off the town from the river and from that time the town declined in importance. Nevertheless it has a busy market square which acts as a focus for the rural community. The square boasts a tall and grand iron clock, erected in 1878 to a design by William Cunliffe. Presumably, on that day all the faces agreed on the correct time!

The Castle Hotel has a distinguished 18th century front; this establishment has associations with Martin King, a dwarf less than four feet high, who died in 1807 from excessive drinking – no doubt to the annoyance of the landlord, who had not only to pay for the funeral but to find a replacement 'boots'. Of more worthy memory, Downham Market was also the birthplace in 1765 of Captain George Manby, who deserves the gratitude of many mariners, since it was he who invented the rocket-fired life-saving rope whose basic design is still employed today.

WHITING & PARTNERS

'. . . the wealthiest Citizen of England of his age, and the founder of 2 Stately Fabricks, the Old Exchange, a kind of Colledge for merchants, and Gresham Colledge, a kind of Exchange for Scholars,'

Thomas Fuller, of Sir Thomas Gresham 1519?–1579

Wells next the Sea

Wells near the sea would be a more accurate name for this town, as it stands at the head of an estuary. It is a thriving port and even to this day cargo ships can be found alongside the quay, unloading cattle cake and fertilizer and taking on grain.

As is the case with many of these delightful north Norfolk ports there is a rich diversity of activity, from the tourist boarding houses and gift shops to the hugely successful fleet of Wells Whelkers, traditional clinker-built boats which brave the dangers of the tidal bar in order to harvest the whelks. It is said that nearly all the whelks sold in England have been landed at Wells.

The town has many streets of narrow winding charm and some pretty flint houses. The loss of this building material is to be regretted, since it has added so much to the character of Norfolk dwellings. Away from the port and beach areas is the Buttlands, a tree-shrouded green of impeccable elegance whose name recalls an earlier, more warlike scene of archers at practice.

The Wells to Walsingham Light Railway, with its new engine *Norfolk Hero* named in deference to Nelson, runs a distance of four miles, making it the longest 10¼" gauge railway in the world and earning it a place in the Guinness Book of Records.

A820 AGM

For a man's house is his castle.

Sir Edward Coke of Mileham 1552–1634

Oxburgh Hall

When Sir Edmund Bedingfield began the construction of Oxburgh Hall in 1482 he must have pondered long and hard about the design, for he was building at a time of great change. There was no point in making a castle, since the improvements in artillery had rendered such defences uncertain at best but the times were very dangerous and property needed protection. The solution was delightfully simple and pleasing to the eye. He built a fortified Hall in brick, with a great tower, placed within the security of a wide moat which enabled him to make his windows large and graceful. While it would never have held off an army, it was quite capable of closing its doors to marauders and rogues.

The enormous gatehouse is possibly the largest in England and certainly it stands proud of all the additions to the site, with its seven storeys of living accommodation. Rumour has it that in 1497 King Henry VII stayed here where now are displayed reminders of a less happy sovereign, Mary Queen of Scots who, with her lady-in-waiting Bess of Hardwick, helped to pass her seventeen years of imprisonment by working a considerable number of remarkably beautiful wall hangings.

The 19th century saw a great deal of enrichment, including a Gothic revival style of chapel by the architect Pugin and the south front view (seen here) with its single storey arcade and lawn leading to the water's edge.

Henry Paston-Bedingfield continues the unbroken line of succession and the Hall with its beautiful gardens is now in the care of the National Trust and open to visitors.

When the sea comes in at Horsey Gap
Without any previous warning,
A swan shall build its rushy nest
On the roof of the Swan at Horning,
And a baldheaded crow, contented and merry
Shall feast on the corpses that float by the ferry!

Trad.

Ranworth Broad

The prospect of over 200 miles of navigable water is enough to excite the hearts of all but the most landlubberly of our island nation and when it is lined by some of the most unspoilt countryside in England, it is little wonder that the Broads are attracting more holiday-makers every year. From the lively bases of Wroxham, Horning and Potter Heigham the boat hiring business is booming, as increasing numbers of people discover the joys and simplicity of cruising.

Ranworth Broad is but one of over 30 large and beautiful expanses of inviting fresh water, offering rest and relaxation to the idle and active alike. Here along the banks of reed, willow and alder a score of nature trails lead the intrepid explorer as far as he wishes to go. Conservation areas and information centres abound.

This is an old part of the Broadland system, for even in 1275 we hear of tithe payments of turf and peat being made to the local monastery. The church of St Helen at Ranworth occupies a Saxon site and has a magnificent painted screen which is the best in the county.

Toll for the brave –
The brave! that are no more:
All sunk beneath the wave,
Fast by their native shore.

William Cowper 1731–1800

Happisburgh

The first problem for the visitor to this coastal village is to match the spelling with the local pronunciation, which is 'Hazeboro'. This is a wild stretch of shoreline, as the number of wrecks charted in these dangerous waters testifies. Running parallel to the land and seven miles distant is a sand bar almost nine miles along; the shipwrecked mariner must hope for swift rescue if he is to survive. The lifeboatmen have won some of their most stirring duels with the elements within sight of this church. For many years indeed, the church tower was the landmark warning sailors of the coastal hazards.

A lighthouse was first built here in 1791 but it was unable to prevent the worst wreck of all in 1801 when HMS *Invincible*, en route to join Nelson's fleet at Copenhagen, foundered and cast the bodies of her crew upon the dunes of the beach. A grassy mound north of the church provided the grave for 119 of them. Memories of war were brought even closer to the village in 1940 when a German bomb missed the church but embedded shrapnel in the aisle pillars of this 15th century building.

The lighthouse to the right of the church continues to guard this stretch of coastline.

Life is very sweet, brother; who would wish to die?

George Borrow 1803–1881

Burnham Overy Staithe

Many of the coastal villages in this part of Norfolk were once thriving ports, but the constant tidal changes left them literally high and dry, never to bustle with river craft again. Burnham Overy Staithe was created after the sea had receeded from this area, so it has an excellent dredged channel and provides ideal sailing conditions for the visitors who often buy and renovate former granaries and maltings, a clue to the former trade of the village.

The name Overy derives from the Old English word 'Offer' meaning a sea bank, and that is the clue to the other pursuit of this region – birdwatching. Close by, the Cockle Path leads the rambler or naturalist to Scolt Head, there to see the Common and Sandwich Tern, while a boat trip to Scolt Head Island beyond reveals even more to study and enjoy.

Here, on an evening, there is a gentle clatter of rigging wires on metal masts and the ceaseless call of the seagulls as they exploit the accidental generosity of another day's boating.

John Crome 1768–1821

I remember meeting my old friend Mr. J. Crome, of Norwich (some of whose landscapes are not surpassed by even those of Gainsborough) with several of his pupils on the banks of the Yare. 'This is our Academy', he cried out triumphantly, holding up his brush.

John Burnet, *Landscape Painting*

Elm Hill, Norwich

We all have an idea of medieval streets which owes more to the stories of Dick Whittington than to reality. Elm Hill is exactly what we like to think Norwich looked like when Falstaff and old Sir Thomas Erpingham strode the lanes in search of a good glass of sack. Many of these houses are of the 16th century and the pretty cobbled street has a warmth and charm which cannot be denied. But this has never been a quiet back street, being one of the main routes down to the city market.

ELM HILL CRAFT SHOP

Index

The River at Thurne (back cover)

This is another of those parts of Norfolk where being on holiday seems to be almost a fulltime occupation. The waterways are witness to constant processions of brightly-coloured craft negotiating awkward bends in the river, with varying degrees of success and seamanship. There are two lovely windmills at Thurne and one can only wonder what their millers would have made of present-day water-borne travellers, who speed past without the use of sails and close their day by sipping expensive drinks from cut-glass tumblers while telling tales of their adventures.